Search and Find
Princesses

Licensed exclusively to Top That Publishing Ltd
Tide Mill Way, Woodbridge, Suffolk, IP12 1AP, UK
www.topthatpublishing.com

0 2 4 6 8 9 7 5 3 1
Manufactured in China

Can you find?

1 kitten

2 vases of flowers

3 cake boxes

4 teddy bears

5 bottles of perfume

The royal day begins

The princess is awake bright and early. Her bedroom is full of princess things. Can you help her to find her favourites?

Can you find?

6 dolls

7 cupcakes

8 books

9 necklaces

10 bows

Can you find?

1 chicken

2 pizzas

3 cakes

4 plates of macarons

5 pies

What's cooking?

Something smells good in the busy palace kitchen! Can you help the princess to spot her favourite kinds of food?

Can you find?

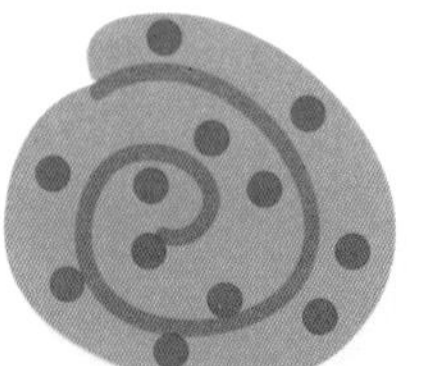

6 Danish swirls

7 loaves of bread

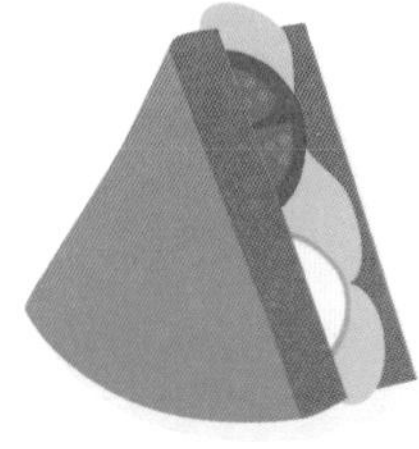

8 sandwiches

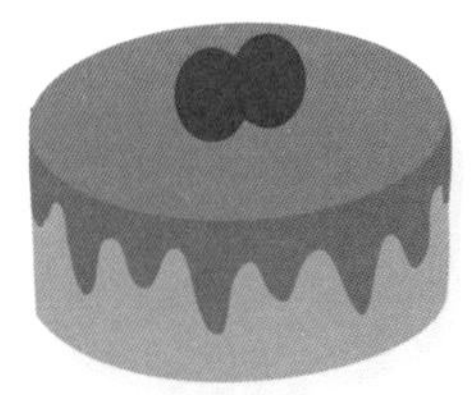

9 purple tarts

10 strawberries

Can you find?

1 watch

2 vests

3 pairs of knickers

4 pairs of boots

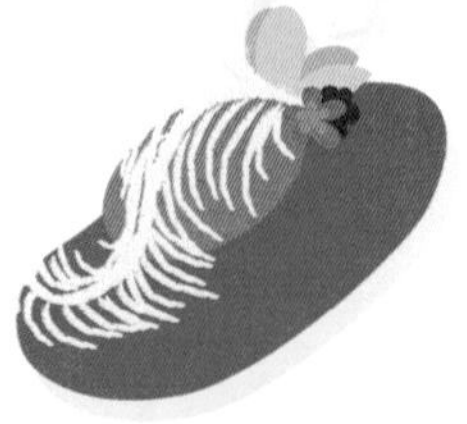

5 pink hats

What to wear?

What will the princess wear today? She has so many clothes to choose from! Help her to find these items so she can make her final selection.

Can you find?

6 handbags

7 pairs of gloves

8 tiaras

9 fans

10 yellow dresses

Can you find?

1 bowl
of eggs

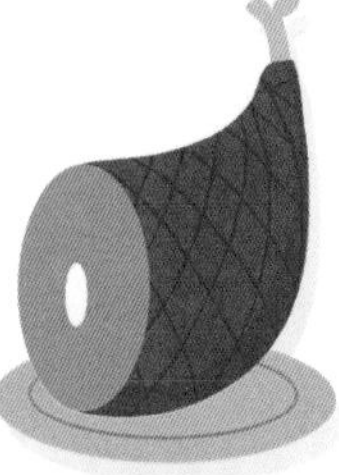

2 hams

3 boxes
of cereal

4 plates
of cheese

5 cartons
of fruit juice

Breakfast for a princess

The hungry princess is ready for a right-royal breakfast. Can you find these items in the smart palace dining room?

Can you find?

6 champagne glasses

7 pots of jam

8 strawberry tarts

9 gold goblets

10 croissants

The royal family … and friends

The princess walks through the royal portrait gallery every day. Can you find these things hidden in the room?

Can you find?

1 kitten

2 lollies

3 pink flowers

4 bumble bees

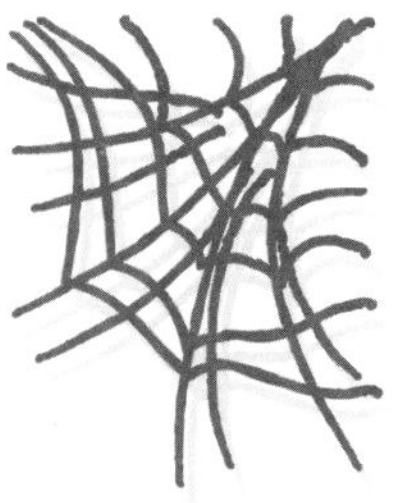

5 spiders' webs

Can you find?

6 pale blue hearts

7 white mice

8 blue birds

9 bows

10 blue butterflies

Can you find?

1 sleeping kitten

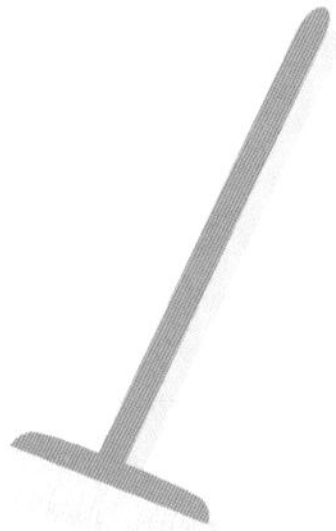

2 brooms

3 ropes

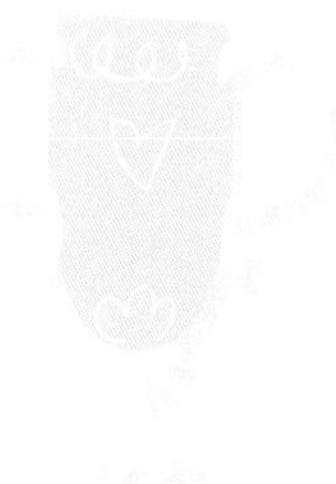

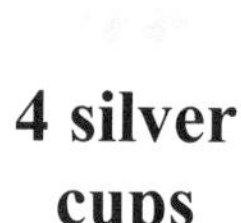

4 silver cups

5 saddles

Getting ready to ride

The princess never misses her daily ride. It's her favourite thing in the world! Can you find all the items that she needs to look after the horses?

Can you find?

6 brushes

7 straw bales

8 red buckets

9 rosettes

10 horseshoes

Can you find?

1 spotty butterfly

2 blue butterflies

3 lilac butterflies

4 red butterflies

5 green butterflies

Beautiful butterflies

The butterfly house is the perfect place for the princess to practise drawing. Can you find all the butterflies fluttering in the scene?

Can you find?

6 aqua butterflies

7 yellow butterflies

8 purple butterflies

9 pink butterflies

10 orange butterflies

Can you find?

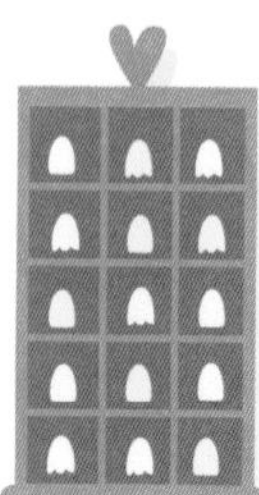

1 thimble display

2 sets of hat boxes

3 sewing boxes

4 pairs of scissors

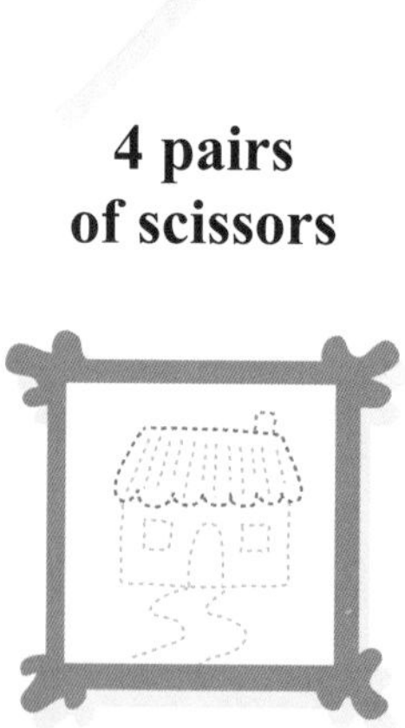

5 cross-stitch pictures

Sewing lessons

Like all princesses, this princess has sewing lessons, but the room is a mess! Can you find the sewing items hidden in the scene and help her to clear up?

Can you find?

6 jars of buttons

7 knitting needles

8 feathers

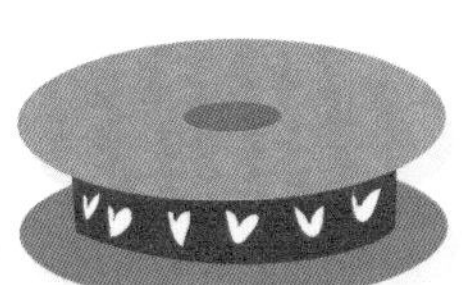

9 rolls of ribbon

10 balls of light blue wool

Can you find?

1 suit of armour

2 crowns

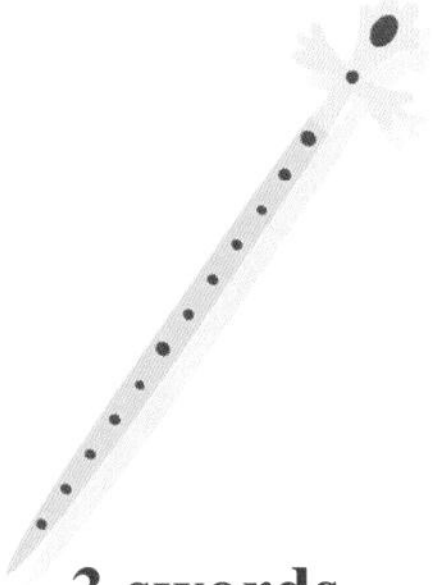

3 swords

4 sceptres

5 tiaras

Royal treasures

Sometimes, the princess sneaks into the treasury to look at the crown jewels. Can you search and find these royal treasures?

Can you find?

6 gold goblets

7 silver candlesticks

8 bead necklaces

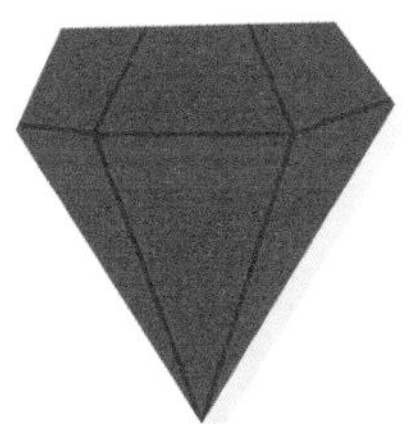

9 rubies

10 orbs

Can you find?

1 dog

2 jackets

3 wigs

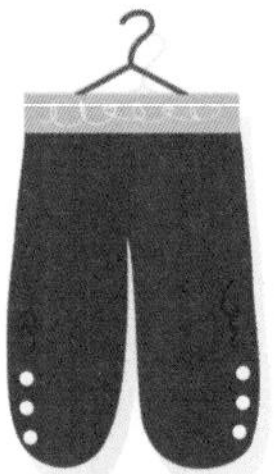

4 pairs of breeches

5 wheels

Royal transport

The carriage room is where the royal coach and equipment are kept. Help the princess to spot these things.

Can you find?

6 harnesses

7 hats

8 feathers

9 horse tiaras

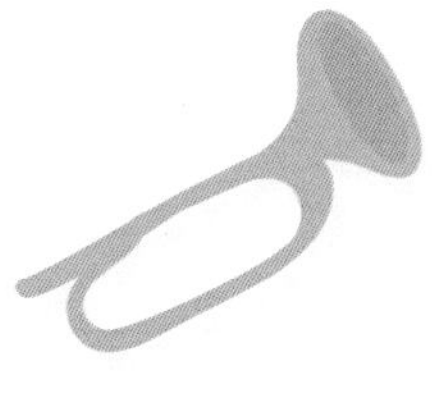

10 bugles

'Smile, please!'

It's time for the royal family and their staff to have their photograph taken. Can you search and find these things in the busy, happy scene?

Can you find?

1 sleeping grey cat

2 white mice

3 maids in grey

4 soldiers in armour

5 coachmen

Can you find?

6 flower displays

7 butlers

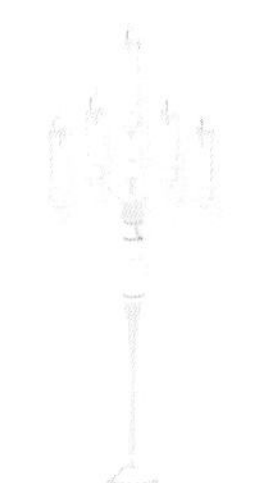

8 candelabras

9 footmen

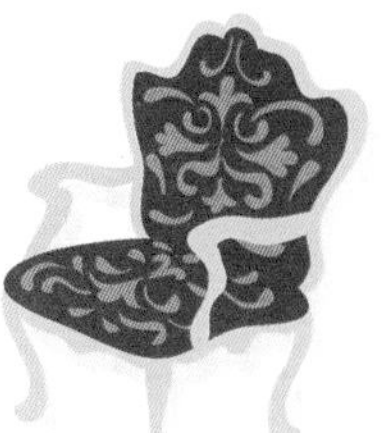

10 chairs

Can you find?

1 sleepy cat

2 ornamental trees

3 bags of soil

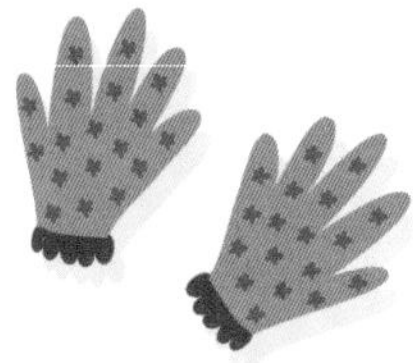

4 pairs of gloves

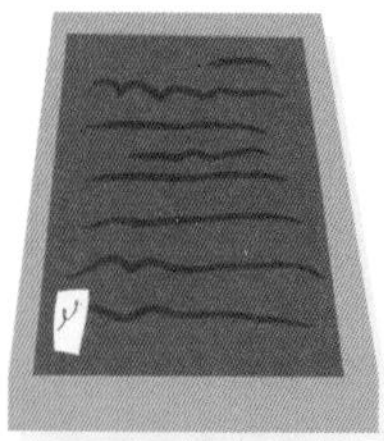

5 seed trays

An indoor garden

The princess loves the palace garden room, full of sweet-smelling flowers. Can you find these things hidden in the pretty scene?

Can you find?

6 small pink flowers

7 blue watering cans

8 flower baskets

9 chairs

10 bumble bees

Fun with friends

The princess and her friends are playing in the games room. Can you spot all these fun things to play with?

Can you find?

1 trampoline

2 black knight chess pieces

3 cricket bats

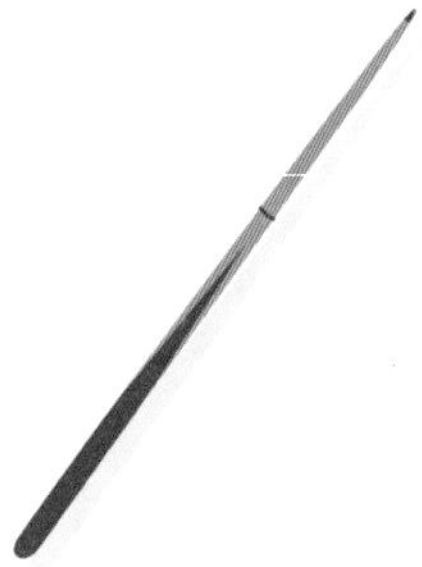

4 pool cues

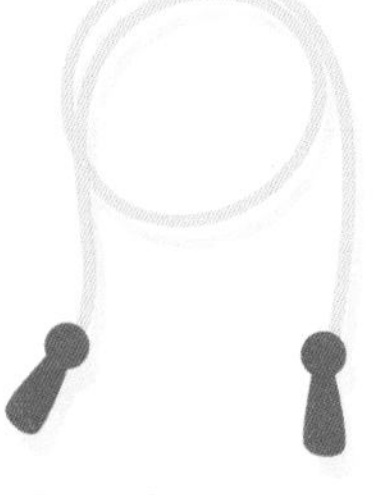

5 skipping ropes

Can you find?

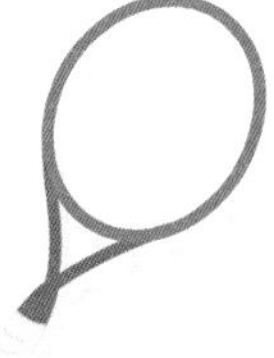

6 rackets

7 croquet mallets

8 table tennis bats

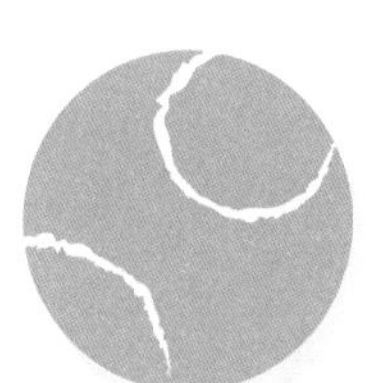

9 tennis balls

10 shuttlecocks

Royal rehearsal

It's time to practise for the royal concert. Can you find these items hidden in the palace music room?

Can you find?

1 barking dog

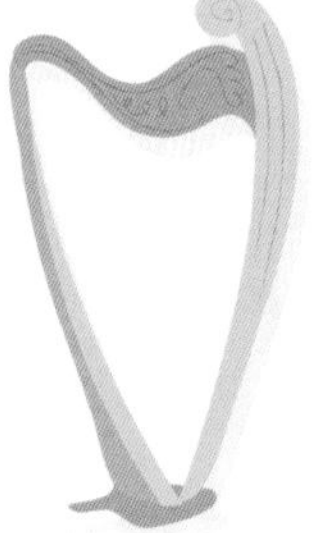

2 harps

3 music stands

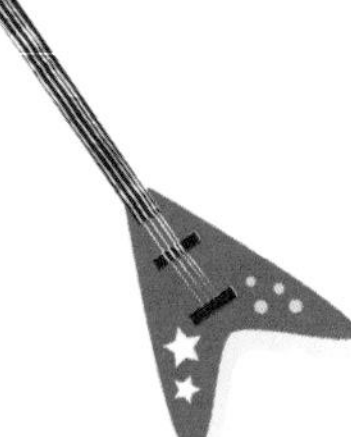

4 electric guitars

5 guitars

Can you find?

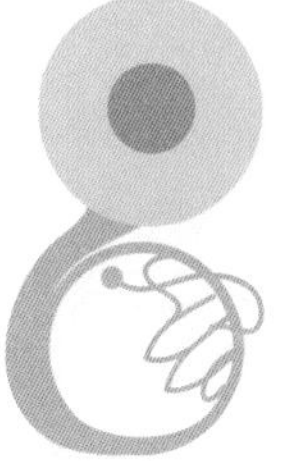

6 sousaphones

7 trumpets

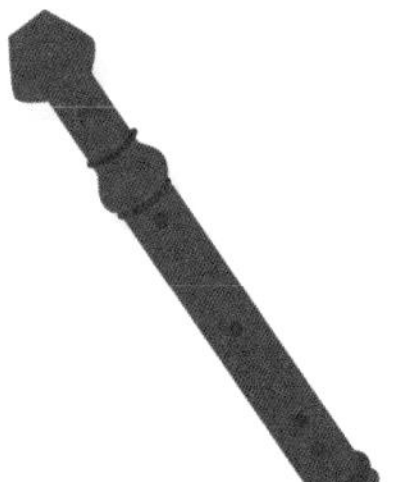

8 purple recorders

9 bugles

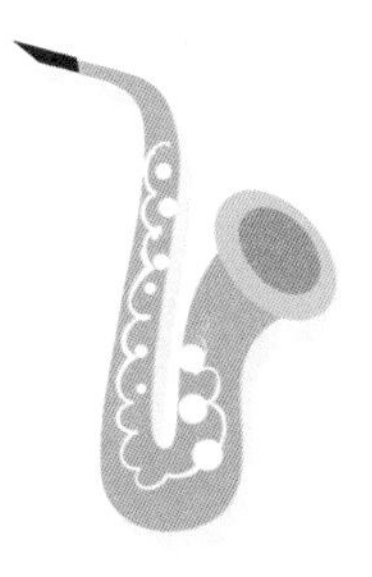

10 saxophones

Can you find?

Teatime!

Princesses love afternoon tea! How many of these things can you find hidden in this sweet scene?

1 chocolate cake

2 plates of macarons

3 gold teapots

4 plates of sandwiches

5 cups and saucers

Can you find?

6 jellies

7 ice cream sundaes

8 cupcakes

9 iced buns

10 plates of grapes

The food cellar

The princess is in the cellar, looking at the food for the royal banquet. How many of these things can you spot?

Can you find?

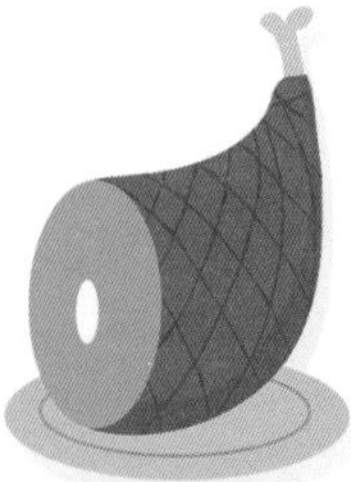

1 ham

2 chocolate cakes

3 plates of cheese

4 roast chickens

5 green jellies

Can you find?

6 plates of sandwiches

7 loaves of bread

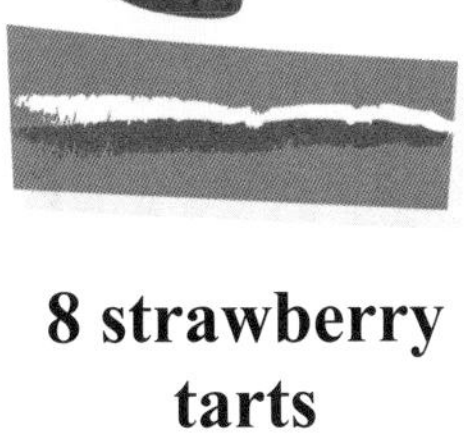

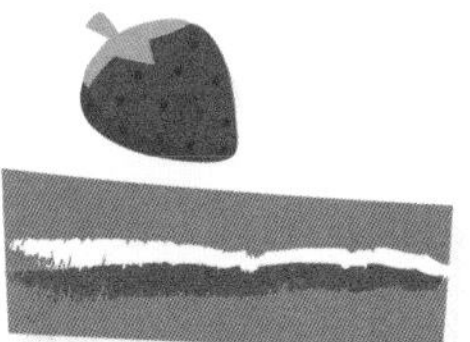

8 strawberry tarts

9 trays of strawberries

10 pies

Can you find?

1 blue bottle of shampoo

2 pink brushes

3 pink ducks

4 piles of towels

5 blue sponges

A relaxing bubble bath

The princess is having a relaxing bubble bath before the grand ball. Can you find these things hidden in the bathroom scene?

Can you find?

6 red
scented oils

7 bags of cotton
wool balls

8 heart-shaped
soaps

9 green
body washes

10 purple
perfumes

Can you find?

1 big pie dish

2 teapots

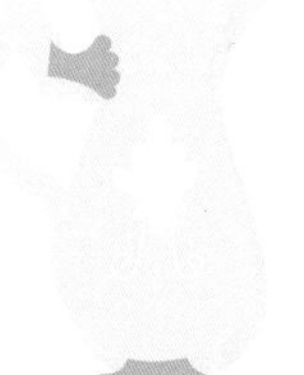

3 jugs

4 cake stands

5 terrines

Busy butlers

The butlers are busy polishing all the royal silver, china and glass. How many of these things can you spot?

Can you find?

6 candelabras

7 silver
ice buckets

8 round
plates

9 tall
glasses

10 teacups
and saucers

Can you find?

1 princess in pink

2 princesses in blue

3 bowing princes

4 princesses in yellow

5 flower displays

Special guests

The guests are arriving for the grand ball. Find all of these people and things at the royal reception.

Can you find?

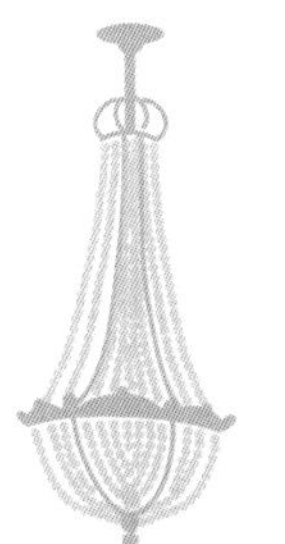

6 chandeliers

7 wall candles

8 statues

9 waiting coachmen

10 drinks trays

Can you find?

1 dish of pears

2 green jellies

3 plates of grapes

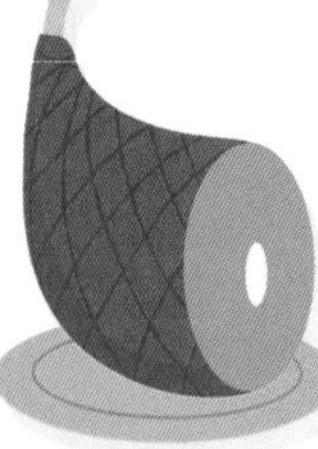

4 hams

5 plates of sandwiches

'Dinner is served'

The table in the banqueting hall is groaning under the weight of all the food. Can you spot these goodies?

Can you find?

6 roast chickens

7 dishes of strawberries

8 pretty trifles

9 ice cream sundaes

10 pink jellies

Can you find?

1 grand piano

2 barking dogs

3 performing princesses

4 grey cats

5 violins

Let's dance!

The guests are dancing and having fun. Can you find these things in the busy ballroom?

Can you find?

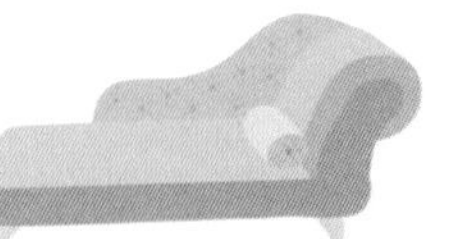

6 golden sofas

7 lost fans

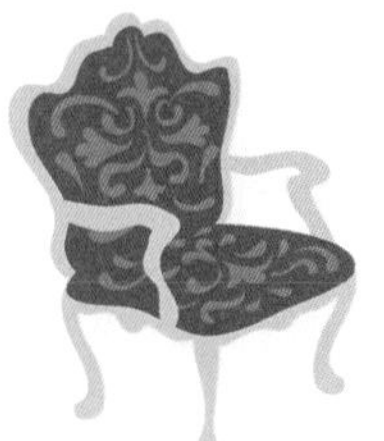

8 chairs

9 maids

10 flower displays

An evening swim

When the party is over, the princess and her friends go swimming in the rooftop pool. What can you spot?

Can you find?

1 floating princess

2 tables

3 butterflies

4 shooting stars

5 candles

Can you find?

6 flower displays

7 piles of red towels

8 green rubber rings

9 beach balls

10 pretty glasses

Sleepy maids

The sleepy maids are worn out! Can you find these things in their big, quiet bedroom?

Can you find?

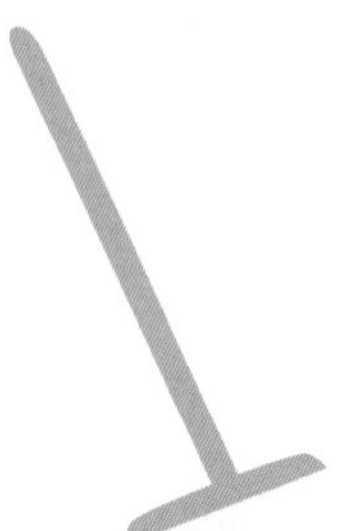

1 pink broom

2 sleepy kittens

3 blue boxes of ribbons

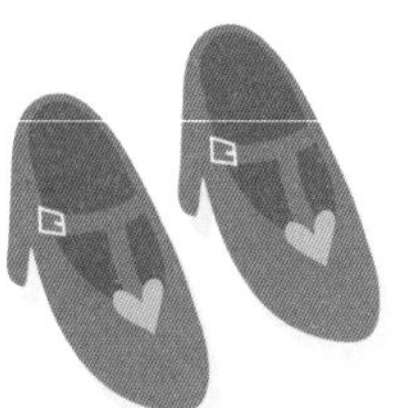

4 pairs of shoes

5 pairs of boots

Can you find?

6 dolls

7 dresses

8 teddies

9 pairs of slippers

10 sleeping caps

Can you find?

1 sleeping kitten

2 wall candles

3 slices of cake

4 bunnies

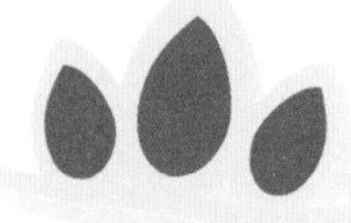

5 tiaras

Royal peace and quiet

The princess loves her little turret room.
Can you find all her favourite things?